ASPECTS OF ROMAN LIF

THE ROMAN

PETER HODGE
Principal teacher of Classics/Lenzie Acadenry

LONGMAN

CONTENTS

F refers the pupil to the folder which accompanies this book.

I. A ROMAN CITY AND ITS HOUSES

Apart from what we know about the city of Rome itself, our knowledge of what life was like for a Roman and the kind of house he lived in would have been surprisingly little had it not been for an event that took place on a summer day in 79 AD. The date was **24th August**, the place **Pompeii**, a city on the western coast of Italy not far from Naples.

Look at the map of Italy on the right and find the following places:

Rome; Naples; Pompeii.

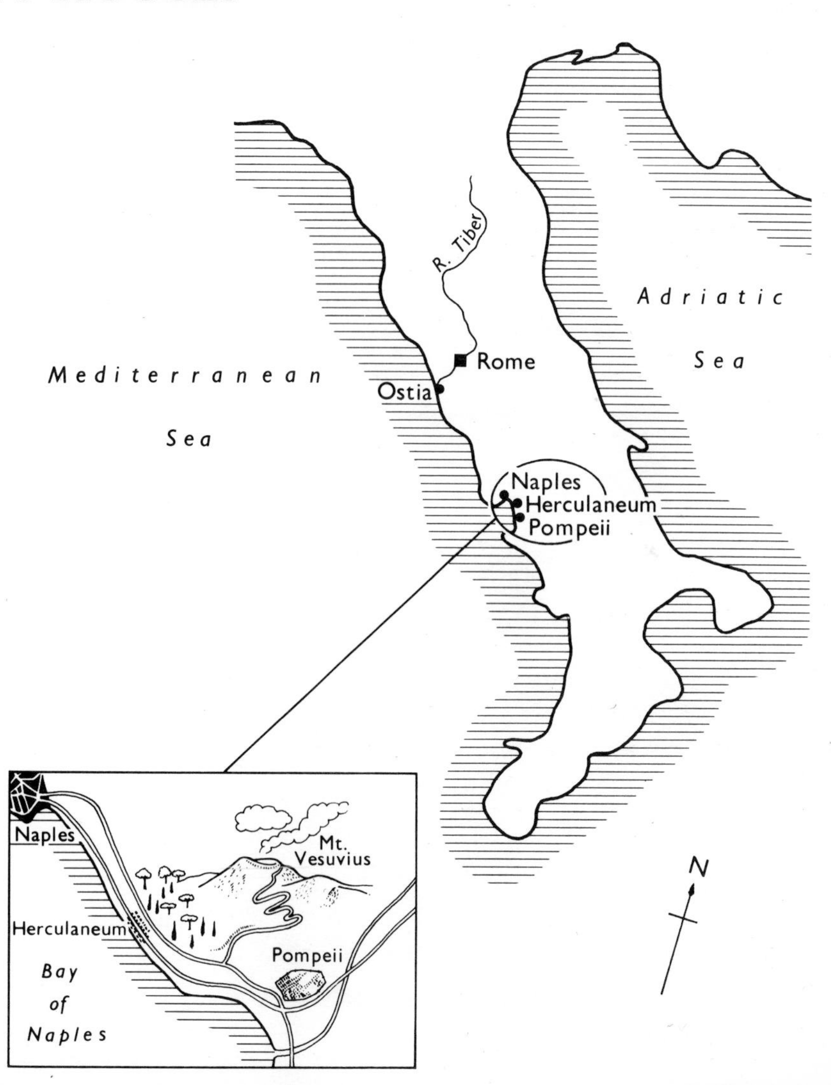

Questions

1 Is Pompeii
   a North of Rome?
   b South of Rome?

2 What is the name of the mountain just to the north of Pompeii?

Mount Vesuvius erupting again in 1944

On the morning of 24th August, 79 AD, a catastrophe occurred which was described by an eye-witness. His name was **Pliny**. Here is part of a letter he wrote to a friend, the historian Tacitus:

'My uncle was at Misenum at the time in charge of the fleet. At about one o'clock in the afternoon of 24th August, my mother pointed out to him a large and unusual looking cloud. . . . At the distance we were from it you couldn't tell exactly which mountain the cloud was rising from (it turned out later to have been Vesuvius), but it looked just like a pine-tree. It shot up into the sky like a tall tree trunk and then spread out into several branches . . ., one moment the colour of it was white, the next it was covered in black spots of what looked like earth or ash.'

PLINY *Epistles* vi. 16.

Now answer the questions below.

[You will find the rest of Pliny's letter in the folder.] F

Questions

1 What was the catastrophe described by Pliny?
2 When did it happen?
3 How do we know that the account of the disaster is true?

There have been many eruptions of Mount Vesuvius since the one described by Pliny.
On the opposite page you can see a photograph taken when Mount Vesuvius was erupting in 1944.
On the right is a photograph showing the volcano when it is dormant (or 'asleep', because it is not actually erupting).

Vesuvius today

A Pompeian dog killed in the eruption and preserved in lava

There were probably about 20,000 people living in Pompeii before the eruption. Most of them escaped, but archaeologists have found about 2000 bodies of people who were not so lucky.
After the eruption Pompeii was buried beneath volcanic ash and mud. It remained buried until 1748 when archaeological excavations were begun, and the fate of the city was unearthed. Since then, more digging has uncovered almost the whole of the city, and we can now see what it must have looked like on the morning the eruption took place.
Look at the street plan of Pompeii below.

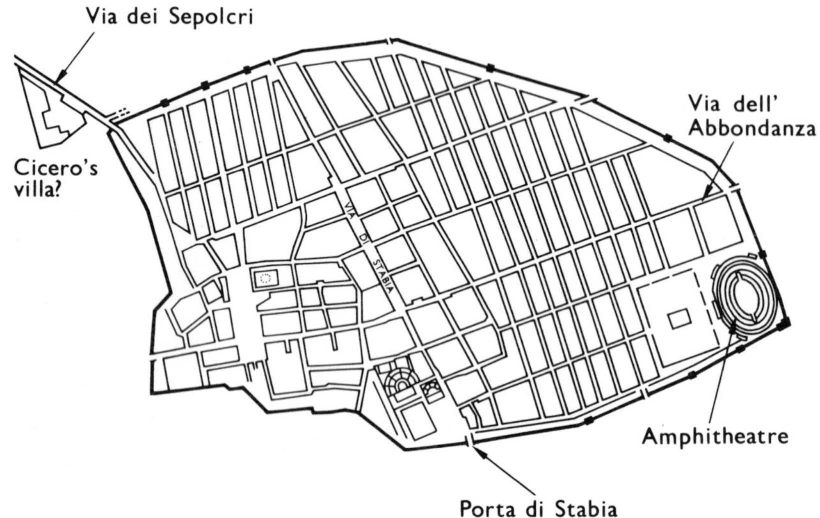

Question

What do you notice about the way the streets and houses were laid out in a Roman city?

Look at the plan of Pompeii and compare the layout of the streets and buildings with that of a large city like Glasgow today which is shown in the plan below.

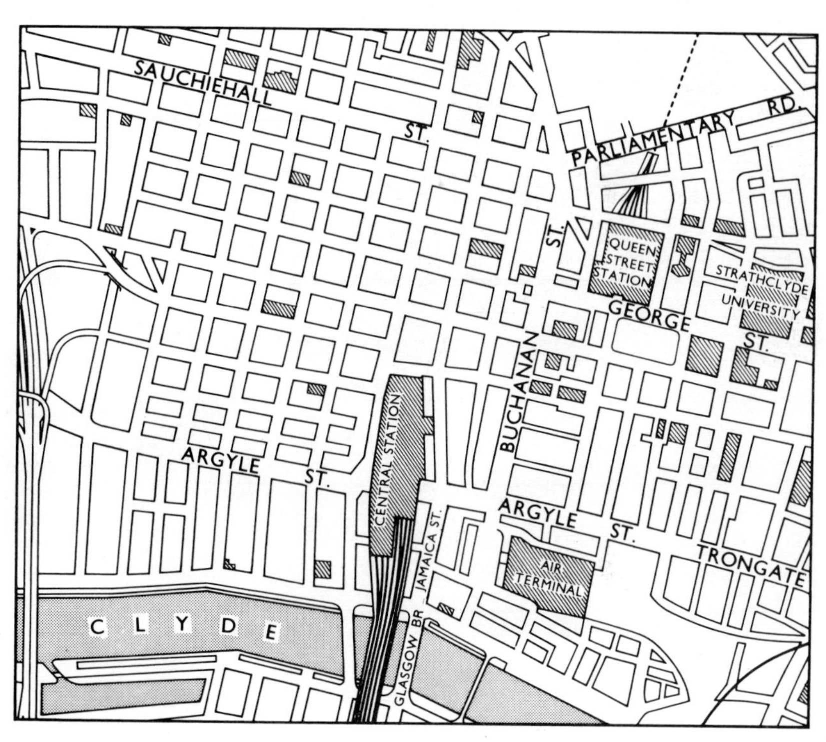

Question

In what way is the layout of the streets and buildings in this city like the plan of a Roman town like Pompeii?

Below is a photograph of one of the main streets in Pompeii. Today this street is called the Via di Stabia (see plan on page 4).

Questions

1 What do you think the Latin word *via* means?

2 Write down three things you notice about the Roman *via* which are labelled in the photograph. (Try to guess what **c** is. Imagine what you might do if it rained hard and you wanted to get from one side of the *via* to the other.)

Just along the coast from Pompeii is the town of **Herculaneum**, which was also buried by the eruption of Mount Vesuvius. The photograph below shows part of the town that has been excavated.

Revision

See how much you can remember of what you have learned so far.

1 Draw a sketch map of Italy and mark on it the following places: Rome; Naples; Pompeii; Mount Vesuvius.
2 Describe briefly in your own words what happened to Pompeii.
3 In what year did the disaster take place?
4 Draw a rough plan to show how the streets and houses were laid out in a Roman city.
5 Write down three things you have learned about Roman streets.

Things to do

1 Find out more information about volcanoes. For example, what causes volcanoes like Mount Vesuvius to erupt? Where else in the world do we find volcanoes? What is the name of the volcano in Sicily? Draw a diagram of a volcano showing what happens when it erupts.
2 Compare the plan of Pompeii with the street plan of a large city near you like London, Birmingham, Manchester, or Edinburgh.

2. INSULAE AND CENACULA

We have already seen that the streets and houses in a Roman city were built to form squares. Each block of buildings was called an **insula**. An *insula* might consist of a number of flats or include one or two larger private houses.
Look at the photographs on the right.

Cenacula along the Via dell'Abbondanza, Pompeii
Block of tenements in Glasgow

Questions

1 What did the Latin word *insula* mean in connection with houses?
2 The two photographs to the right show examples of an *insula* consisting of a number of *cenacula*. What do you think a *cenaculum* was? (Choose the answer you think correct.)
   a A private house
   b A tenement flat

The **cenaculum** it seems was by far the commonest type of dwelling in Roman cities. It was the home of poorer families and slaves. Each family had its own *cenaculum*.
The *insulae* in Pompeii were probably no more than two storeys high, but in other cities like Rome and Ostia the *insulae* were often three or four storeys high, and we know from some records of blocks of flats that were built even higher in the time of Augustus. In fact Augustus had to pass a law limiting the height of insulae to 20 metres (STRABO V. iii. 7).

It is known that by the fourth century AD, there were about 46,600 blocks of these flats in Rome and only about 1800 private houses. This means that for every private house there were 26 blocks of flats.

Building *insulae* in Rome

Question

Were there more
- **a** tenement flats
- **b** private houses

in Rome?

Below is a photograph of a reconstruction of an *insula* at Ostia (which was the port of Rome) consisting of many *cenacula*.

Questions

1 Who lived in the *cenacula*?
  a The rich
  b The poor and slaves

2 Look at the photograph above carefully. How high were these flats originally as far as we can tell?
  a Two storeys
  b Three or four storeys
  c Four or more storeys

Tall blocks of flats today also sometimes collapse. Here James Callaghan inspects the Ronan Point high rise block of flats that collapsed in 1968

Life for families living in the *cenacula* was rather overcrowded and uncomfortable. Most had no running water or sanitation, and in addition to the discomfort there were frequent dangers. Below is an extract from a piece of satirical verse written by the poet **Juvenal** round about the end of the first century AD:

'We're living in a city that's propped up with little more than matchsticks: and they're the only way the rent-man can keep his tenants from falling out, as he plasters over the gaps in the cracks and tells them not to worry when they go to bed (even if the place *is* just about to fall around them!). It's wrong for people to have to live in fear of house-fires and buildings collapsing all the time. Right now your next door neighbour is calling for the fire-brigade and moving his bits and pieces while your own wee garret is smoking and you know nothing about it. If the folk at the bottom of the stairs panic, the chap who's trapped and the last to burn is the one in the top attic just under the roof that keeps the rain off himself and the pigeon's nest. . . . Poor old Joe Bloggs didn't have a bean, but he lost everything he had—and the worst of it is that nobody will give him a meal or a roof over his head when he's in rags and begging for a crust of bread. But if the mansion of one of your millionaires collapses, the whole city thinks it's a catastrophe—the man's wife gets hysterical, the bigwigs are terribly upset and the magistrates adjourn court-cases. Everyone gets really het up about the fire, but nobody calls the fire-brigade . . .!'

JUVENAL *Satires* i. 3. 193ff

Questions

1 What kinds of danger is Juvenal describing?

2 What does he mean when he says that the city is 'propped up with little more than matchsticks'?

A back court view of some old tenements in Glasgow

Questions

1 What problems is the woman describing in the passage above?
2 In what ways are the flats in the picture like the Roman tenements you have seen?

Compare what you have just read about life in a Roman tenement with the following extract in which a woman describes her life in poor housing conditions in 1970.

'See this wall here—that crack only appeared since the house next door came down. The master of works says that's the worst bit—over there where the other building used to be.
He says that by the bed there is nothing. But that crack is right through to the box-room. It's all falling apart. They put this metal in and said if it moves it'll crack. I'm frightened, in fact I'm terrified to sleep in the bed. . . . This patch here means the rain's coming in again. The two children have to sleep here.'

from *'Condemned'*: a SHELTER Report on Housing and Poverty, 1971.

And here are some more extracts from other Roman writers:

'Novius is a neighbour of mine—I can lean out of the window and touch him with my hand!'

MARTIAL i. 86.

'The Marcian canal roars past my window—and yet there's no running water in the house.'

MARTIAL ix. 18.

'Crassus also noticed that fires and buildings collapsing were common, everyday occurrences in Rome because of the size of the buildings and their closeness to one another.'

PLUTARCH *Life of Crassus* 2.

As with many modern tenements, it was quite common to find the ground floor of an *insula* consisting not of apartments but **tabernae** where all kinds of food and provisions could be bought.
Look at the photograph below.

A butcher's shop

Question

What do you think the Latin word *taberna* means?

Revision

Now test yourself on what you have just learned.

1 What is an *insula*?
2 What is the modern equivalent of the Roman *cenaculum*?
3 Who lived in a *cenaculum*?
4 What was the commonest kind of house in Rome and Ostia?
5 How many storeys high were the flats in Ostia?
6 How many storeys did the tenements in Pompeii have?
7 What is the name of the Roman writer who wrote a humorous description of life in Roman flats?
8 What might you find on the ground floor of a block of flats in a Roman city?

Things to do

1 Draw a picture or make a model of an *insula* consisting of *cenacula*.
2 If you live in or near a block of flats, draw a picture of it, and compare it with the photographs on pages 10 and 11.
3 Imagine you are a Roman living in a tenement flat.
Either write a description of what life is like for you
Or make up a scene in which you are complaining to the landlord about the state of the flat.

3. THE DOMUS

Although we have seen that there were tenements in Pompeii, these were not as common in Pompeii as they were in larger cities like Rome and Ostia. Pompeii was a seaside resort and so was different from Rome where there was a great housing problem. Pompeii seems to have had more private houses than tenements.

The private house or **domus** was the home of the middle class and rich families. On the right is a photograph of the front of a *domus* in the Via dell' Abbondanza. It belonged to a man called Caius Secundus.

Questions

1 What three things do you notice about the front of this house that makes it different from the *cenacula*? (Look back at page 9.)
   a What about the number of storeys?
   b What kind of windows can you see?
   c What about the doorway?

2 What kind of man do you think Caius Secundus was?

Caius Secundus' house, like many private houses, was only one storey high, although some had a second storey, as you can see from the photograph here.
The *domus* faced right onto the street and usually had only one or two small windows at the front. The front entrance had a porch over it.
Caius Secundus was probably quite well off. He was rich enough to have his own house, but not wealthy enough to own a large one.

House of the Gran Sacerdote, Pompeii. This house has two storeys

The Romans got their ideas for building private houses from the Greeks who colonised Southern Italy. The earliest kind of *domus* was built on the same kind of plan as a Greek house.
Look at the picture and plan of the simplest kind of *domus* below.

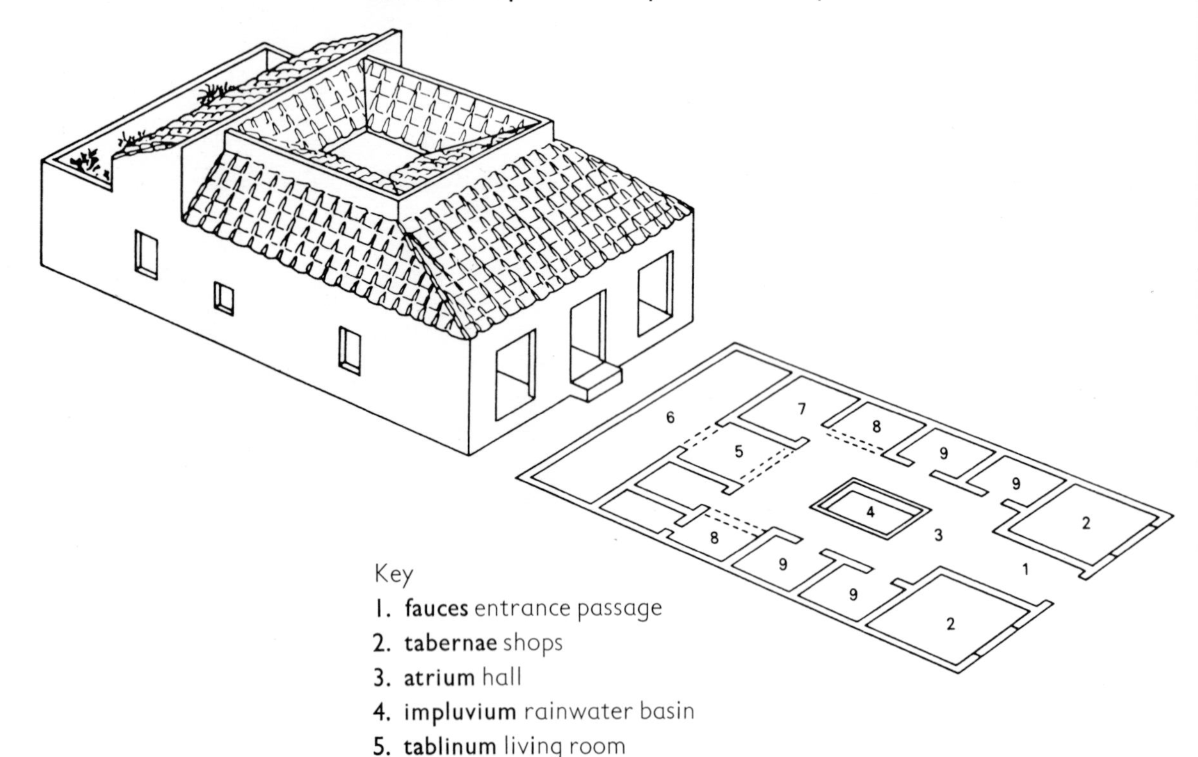

Key
1. **fauces** entrance passage
2. **tabernae** shops
3. **atrium** hall
4. **impluvium** rainwater basin
5. **tablinum** living room
6. **hortus** garden
7. **triclinium** dining room
8. **alae** side-rooms
9. **cubiculum** bedroom

Questions

1 What shape was this house?
2 What was in the middle of it?

The Romans later added a courtyard and garden at the back of the house with several rooms round it as you can see in this picture.

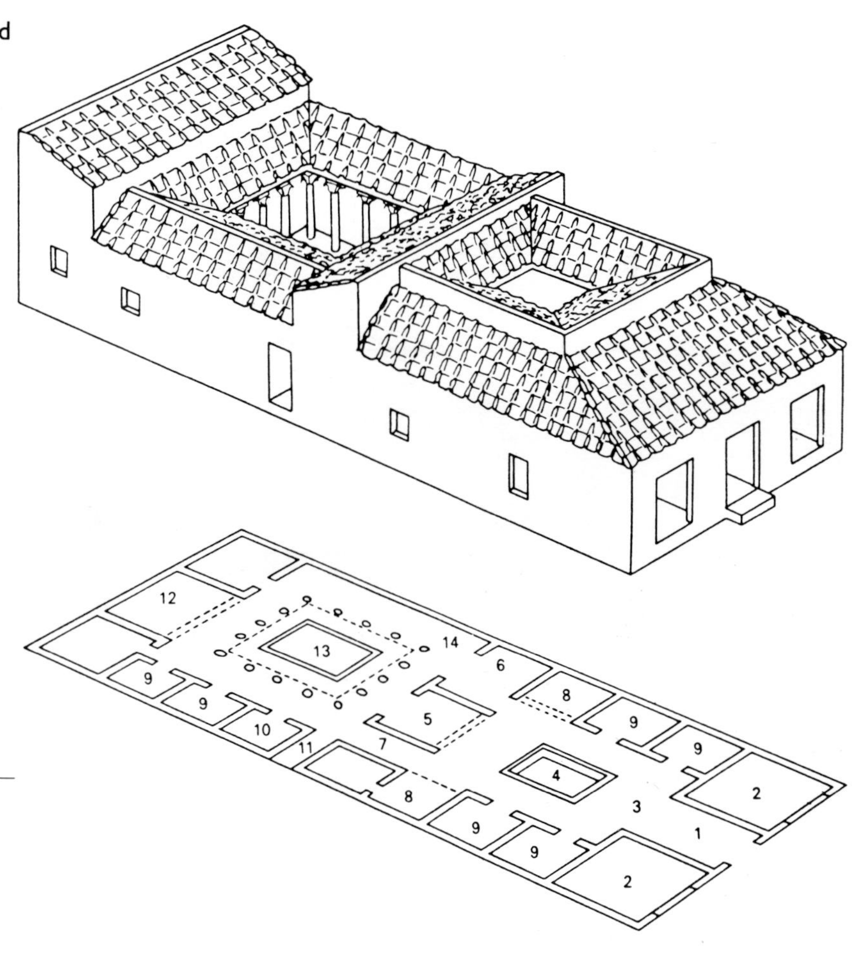

1. **fauces** entrance passage
2. **tabernae** shops
3. **atrium** hall
4. **impluvium** rainwater basin
5. **tablinum** living room
6. **triclinium** dining room
7. **andron** passage
8. **alae** side-rooms
9. **cubiculum** bedroom
10. **culina** kitchen
11. **posticum** back-door
12. **exhedra** garden-room
13. **piscina** fishpond (or **hortus** garden)
14. **peristylium** garden-court

Questions

1 Which part of this *domus* was the early part?
a front part
b back part
2 What did the Romans add to the Greek house?
3 What was the *atrium* (number 3 on the plan)?
4 What was the *peristylium* (number 14 on the plan)?

The *domus* did not have a garden at the front. Instead it faced onto a courtyard at the back, which was enclosed within the walls of the house. It gave the people living in it greater privacy.
Below are two photographs of a modern house which is very similar in plan to the basic plan of a Roman *domus*.

Front view

Back view

Questions

What two things do you notice about these houses which make them like a *domus*?

At the entrance to the *domus* was a small porch (**vestibulum**) which led off the street. The front door (**ianua**) was set back from the street by this porch. As you stepped into the porch, you might find a mosaic like the one in the photograph below.

Questions

1 What was the *vestibulum*?

2 Where was the front door of a Roman house
  a In front of the vestibulum?
  b Behind the vestibulum?

3 What is the modern equivalent of 'cave canem'?

After stepping inside the front door, you entered a passage **(fauces)** which led into a large hall called the **atrium**.
Look at the plan on page 19 and find the *atrium*. Below is a photograph of the *atrium* in the House of the Lovers in Pompeii.

Questions

1 What do you notice about the roof? Why do you think it was like this?
2 How is the roof of the *atrium* supported in this picture?

The *atrium* was open to the sky. The tiled roof of the house sloped down on four sides to the **compluvium**, or hole in the roof of the *atrium*. This was to let in light and air. But it also let in the rain in bad weather. And so in the centre of the floor of the *atrium* was an **impluvium**, or shallow trough, which caught the rainwater. The water was then led off by a pipe to a tank underneath the house.

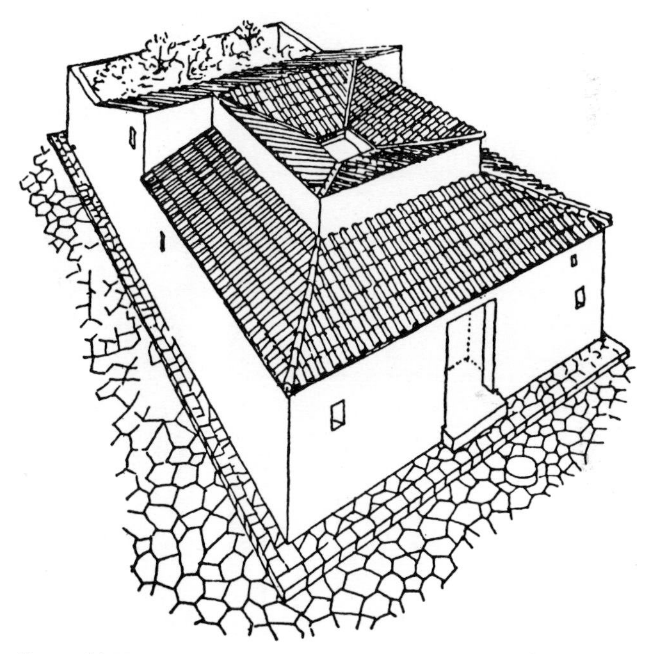

Question

What is the name for the trough in the *atrium* that caught the rain?

a *Compluvium* ?

b *Impluvium* ?

The roof of the *atrium* was supported in different ways. Each type was given a name. The 3 main kinds of *atrium* were

a Atrium **Tuscanicum**: the roof was supported by rafters or wooden beams, and not by pillars.

b Atrium **Tetrastylum**: the roof was supported by 4 pillars.

c Atrium **Corinthium**: the roof was supported by 6 or more pillars, and the *compluvium* was much larger.

Below are photographs of two different types of *atrium*. Look at them carefully and label each with its correct name.

Look back at page 22. What kind of *atrium* is this?

1

2

Originally the *atrium* was the centre of family life. It was the room where the family hearth or fireplace stood. It probably got its name from the Latin word *ater*=black. The *atrium* was the room blackened by the soot and smoke from the fireplace. Gradually, however, as houses became larger the *atrium* was used for entertaining visitors and friends.

Iron Age hut
found on the Palatine Hill, Rome
(8th century BC)

On the left is a picture showing the earliest type of dwelling in Rome. These huts probably had a hole in the roof for the smoke from the fire to escape.

Questions

1 What was the *atrium* originally used for?
2 How did it probably get its name?
3 What was it used for later?

In the earliest Roman houses, the *atrium* was the main room of the *domus*. In it were the family safe (**arca**) and the shrine or altar to the gods who protected the house and family. These gods were called the **lares** and **penates**, and the shrine itself was called a **lararium**. Below is a photograph of a *lararium*.

A metal safe (*arca*) from Pompeii, used for keeping valuable objects and important documents

Questions

1 What was a *lararium*?
2 Why did the Romans worship the *lares* and *penates*?
3 In which room of a Roman house would you find a *lararium*?

The Romans apparently did not fill their houses with furniture as many people do nowadays. A large room like the *atrium* usually had a table and a couch or chairs. Tables were made of wood, marble, or bronze as in the case of the table here, and were often beautifully carved.

Three-legged table from Pompeii.

Questions

1 What kind of furniture did the Romans have in their houses?
2 What kind of lighting did they have?

For lighting the Romans used oil lamps which could be carried from room to room, or mounted on a **candelabrum** like the one shown here.

The room in which the Roman family lived and where only special friends of the family were allowed was the **tablinum**. It was situated on the far side of the *atrium* opposite the hall and faced out onto the courtyard or garden at the back. This courtyard was called the **peristylium**.

Below is a photograph taken looking from the *atrium* of a large *domus* into the *tablinum*. In the background you can just see the *peristylium*.

Questions

1 What was the *tablinum*?
  a Living-room?
  b Room for entertaining guests?
2 Did the *tablinum* have a door?
3 What did the *tablinum* look onto at the back of the house?
  a Atrium?
  b Peristylium?

From the *tablinum* one looked out onto the **peristylium** or courtyard at the back.
Below is a photograph of the *peristylium* of a large house in Pompeii.

Peristyle in the House of the Vettii, Pompeii, showing a sundial in the foreground

Questions

1 What do you notice in the centre of the *peristylium*?
2 What stood all round the *peristylium*?
3 What did these support?
4 What is the modern word for the *peristylium* of a Roman house?

Revision

Below is a simplified plan of a *domus*. Test your knowledge of the rooms so far by writing down (**a**) the Latin name of the room or part, and (**b**) the modern equivalent.

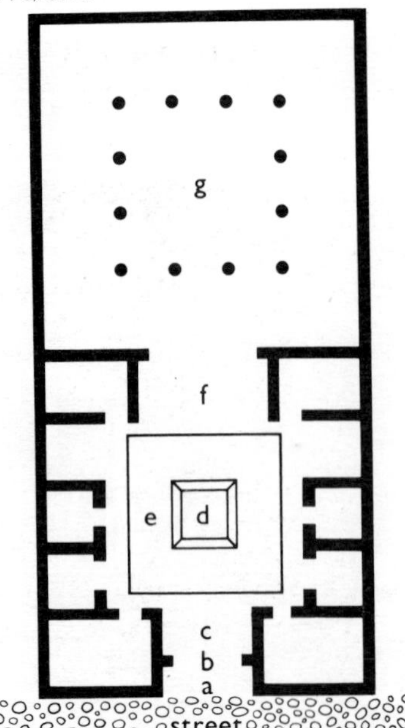

	Latin word	Modern equivalent
a =	______________	______________
b =	______________	______________
c =	______________	______________
d =	______________	______________
e =	______________	______________
f =	______________	______________
g =	______________	______________

Check your answers with the plan on page 46.

Things to do

1. Draw a picture or plan of a Roman *domus* from the plan on page 46 and mark in the various parts.
2. Find out more about Roman furniture from books in your school library.
   You may find the following useful:
   F R Cowell *Everyday Life in Ancient Rome* pp 23-29
   U E Paoli *Rome: Its People, Life and Customs* pp 78-84
   Draw and label (in Latin if you can) pictures of some items of Roman furniture.
3. Imagine you are a Roman housewife (or her husband) and have just moved into a new house. Write a conversation in which you give the removal men instructions as to where to put the furniture. (You might have difficulty in getting them to do what you want!)

Look at the plan of the *domus* again on page 19.
On the right of the *tablinum* and next to it was the **triclinium** where the family ate their meals. The *triclinium* was entered by a door from the *atrium*.
Below is a photograph of a *triclinium* as it is today, and on the left an artist's impression of what a Roman dinner party might have been like.

Questions

1 What is the modern equivalent of the *triclinium*?
2 What do you notice about the seating arrangement?
3 What is in the centre?

The idea of eating while lying on one elbow or reclining was originally a Greek habit which was introduced into Italy with the spread of Greek culture in the third century BC. Before this, the Romans used to eat in the *atrium* or in the *tablinum*, and it was only later that they built a special dining-room.
The furniture of the *triclinium* consisted of a table **(mensa)** which was often square, although later we find round dining-tables, and three couches. Each couch **(lectus)** could seat three people.
There were cushions for each person to lean on while eating, as you can see here.

Table and couches with cushions and table napkins

Questions

1 Where did the Romans eat their meals originally?
2 When was the custom of eating while reclining introduced? And by whom?
3 How many people could be seated round the *mensa* at one time?

Each person sat in a special place at the table, depending on how important a person he was and whether he was a member of the family or not.
The head of the family sat at the TOP of the Bottom Couch **(lectus imus)** and the most important guest sat on his left at the BOTTOM of the Middle Couch **(lectus medius)**. The Top Couch was called the **lectus summus**.

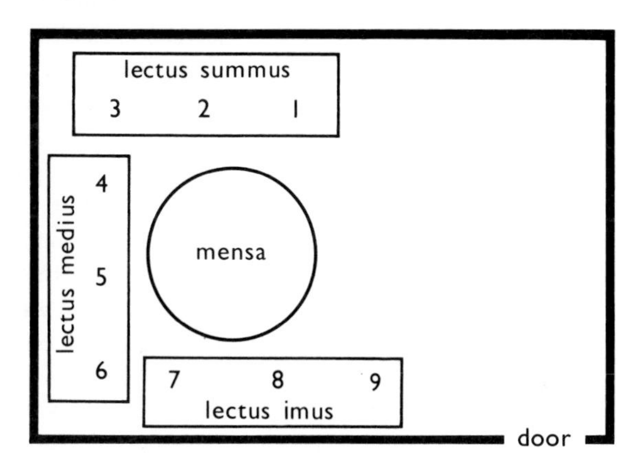

Questions

1 Write down the number of the place where
  a The head of the family sat.
  b The most important guest sat.
2 Where was the top couch?
  a Next to the door.
  b Opposite the door.
3 Where was the bottom couch?

Seating arrangements at a dinner party

'I was at the top couch, and next to me was Viscus, a chap from Thurii. Below him, if I remember, were Varius and Vibidius with Servilius Balatro—two blokes Maecenas had just brought along. Above our host was Nomentanus and below him Porcius, a proper pig.'

HORACE Satires II.8.

The Romans used the *triclinium* for dinner (**cena**). The *cena* was the main meal of the day, equivalent to our dinner or supper, and usually started in the late afternoon round about four o'clock. If it was a large banquet, it might last several hours.
In the following extract, the poet Horace is describing a lavish dinner given by a man called Nasidienus Rufus who was rather a snob:

'For first course there was roast boar from Lucania with spicy radishes and lettuce to tickle a tired stomach, fish, fish-pickle and tartar sauce. When these dishes had been cleared away, a boy in a mini-skirt wiped the maple table clean with a purple napkin. Then in came an Indian carrying the Caecuban wine. . . . The mob—that's us ordinary folk—had poultry, fish and oysters served up with the livers of plaice and turbot which gave them an unusual flavour. . . . Next they brought in a lamprey on a dish with prawns swimming round it in a sauce made from olive oil, caviar, wine and pepper. . . . In the middle of all this the tapestries on the wall came crashing down onto the dish in clouds of dust! Then in came slaves carrying an enormous dish on which there were pieces of stork (seasoned with salt and flour), goose liver, hares' legs, blackbirds' breasts and pigeons. Our host began to tell us their life histories, worst luck. We got our own back on him though—we scarpered!'

HORACE Satires II.8.

Questions

1 What did the Romans call dinner or supper? When did it start?
2 How many different dishes or kinds of food does Horace mention?
3 Do you think he is being serious?

In the ordinary Roman house, the **culina**, or kitchen, was little more than a stove or oven tucked away out of sight of the rest of the house. In the larger *domus* it might include a brick oven and a sink for washing up in, although to judge from some of the banquets that were held the rich must have had bigger and better kitchens in which to prepare some of the exotic dishes like those on the menu below.

Menu

Whole lobster garnished with asparagus

Corsican mullet

Goose liver
Spring chicken
(the size of a goose!)
Roast boar
Truffles and Mushrooms

Apples
(the scent of them alone is a feast in itself)

From JUVENAL *Satires* v. 80ff

Fires appear to have been fairly common in Roman kitchens. Horace says there had been a fire in the kitchen of a friend's house when he was dining there:

'The stove had overturned and flames were running through the old kitchen and rapidly threatening to lick the roof.'

HORACE *Satires* i. 5. 73–74

Questions

1 What was the *culina*?
2 How does it compare with its modern equivalent?

Revision

1 What was a *triclinium?*
2 How many people could the average *triclinium* seat?
3 How did the Romans eat their meals? Where did they get this custom from?
4 What did the Romans call dinner or supper? When did it usually start?
5 What was a *culina?*

Things to do

1 Draw a plan or picture of a Roman dining room showing the seating arrangements.
2 Find out about the kinds of food, wine and cooking utensils the Romans had, and write a paragraph about them.
You may find the following books useful:
F Carcopino *Daily Life in Ancient Rome* pages 287-300.
U E Paoli *Rome: Its People, Life and Customs* pages 86-98.
3 Look at the folder and find more descriptions of Roman food and recipes. Plan a menu for a dinner party F
You will find more information about Roman meals in *Roman Family Life* pages 49-53.
4 Pretend you are a Roman of modest income and have been invited to dinner at a rich man's house. Describe the meal, using the extract on page 34 and the information in the folder to help you.

Along the two sides of the *atrium* in the Roman *domus* were the **cubicula** where the family slept. Each *cubiculum* had a door which opened onto the *atrium*, and in one corner of the room was a recess with a high bed.

Below is a picture of a Roman bed. It would have had a kind of mattress and cushions on it as well as bedclothes.

Questions

1 What was a *cubiculum*?

2 Were the *cubicula*

  a Upstairs?

  b On the ground floor?

At the end of the *atrium* on either side was an open recess called an **ala**. The use of these *alae* is not clear. They probably came from the early *domus* and were used to keep the busts and statues of family ancestors (**imagines**). These *imagines* or statues were almost equivalent to our family portraits or photograph albums.
The Romans showed great respect for their ancestors as we can see from the following extract:

'Portraits modelled in wax were arranged, each in its own niche, as images to accompany the funeral processions of the family. When someone died, every member of the family who had ever lived was always present at the funeral.'
PLINY THE ELDER *Natural Histories* xxxv. 2

A man holding the busts of his ancestors

Questions

1 What were the *alae*?
2 What would you expect to find in the *alae* of a Roman *domus*?

Round the **peristylium** or courtyard at the back were various rooms.

Along one side there were often bedrooms which opened onto the courtyard and were used in summer. In large houses there was sometimes another dining-room which was used in the summer time for meals.

At the far end of the courtyard, opposite the living-room, was a garden room **(exhedra)** for entertaining guests on fine days.

In the middle of the courtyard there was often a garden **(hortus)** or an ornamental pool **(piscina)**.

Peristyle in the House of the Vettii in Pompeii, showing the *exhedra*, garden and ornamental statues.

Questions

1 What rooms would you find in the rear of a *domus?*

2 What do you notice in the middle of the courtyard in the photograph?

Below is the plan of a very large *domus* in Pompeii called the House of the Faun.
Look carefully at the plan and answer the questions.

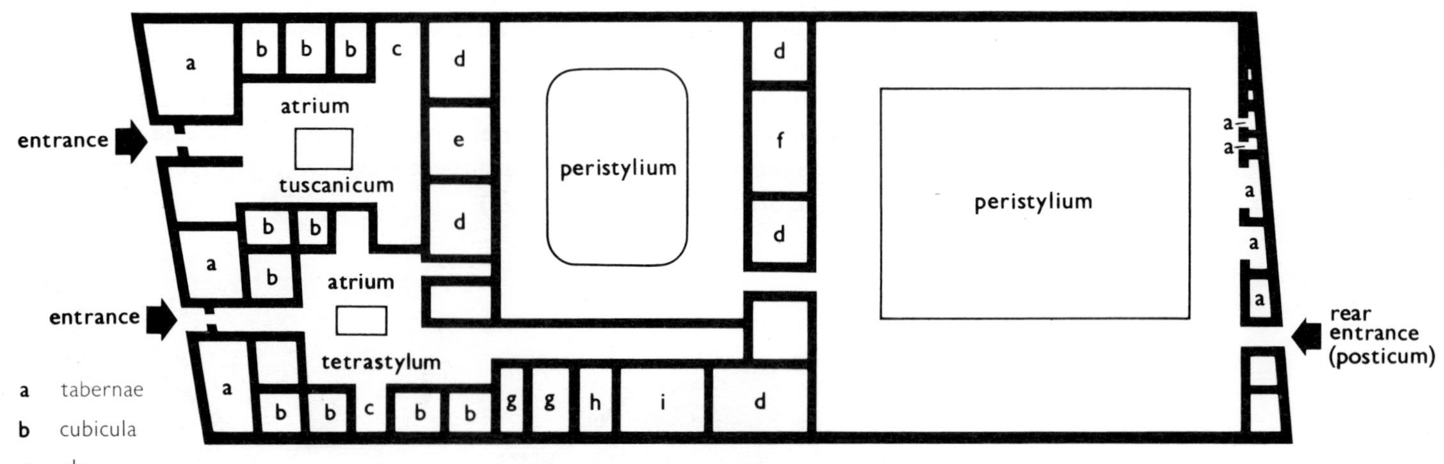

a tabernae
b cubicula
c ala
d triclinium
e tablinum
f exhedra
g stables
h bathroom
i culina

Questions

1 What kind of person lived here, do you think?
  a Middle class family?
  b Rich family?
2 How many *atria* did this house have?
3 How many dining-rooms can you see?
4 How many courtyards or patios?
5 Did it have a bathroom?

Only the very rich could afford a *domus* the size of the one shown on page 40. This particular house probably belonged to P. Sulla, the nephew of one of the consuls in the second century BC. It had a large kitchen and a bathroom, something only the very rich could afford. Most Romans had no bathroom at all in their houses. If they wanted to have a bath, they had to go to the **thermae** or public baths.

On the right is a reconstruction of another large house in Pompeii. It is called the House of Pansa and we are looking at it from the back of the house.

Notice the **posticum** or back door, as well as the side door. It was a useful way of escape it seems if you did not want to see someone who called!

The poet Horace talks about the owner of a house

'slipping out by the side door to escape a visitor who was waiting in the atrium.'
HORACE *Epistles* i. 5. 31

Questions

1 What was the *posticum?*
2 How many storeys high was the House of Pansa according to the picture above?
3 Where did most Romans have to go if they wanted a bath?

The rich who could afford large houses often spared no expense in decorating the rooms with mosaics on the floors, wall paintings, and expensive statues and ornaments, as you can see from the photographs here and on the opposite page.
Sometimes the picture was of a household scene; sometimes it showed a heroic battle scene or a story about the gods and goddesses.

Mosaic of a cat killing a partridge, and some ducks, from Pompeii

A wall painting from a house in Rome illustrating a story from the life of Ulysses

In Pompeii you can still see some of the beautiful wall paintings like those in the photograph below. This is one of the rooms in the House of the Vettii.

Questions

1 What kind of decorations did the Romans have in their houses?
2 In what kind of house do you find these decorations?

Revision

How well do you know what you have learned about the *domus*? Look at the plan below and write down the names of the rooms and parts which are lettered with their modern equivalents. Then answer the questions on page 45.

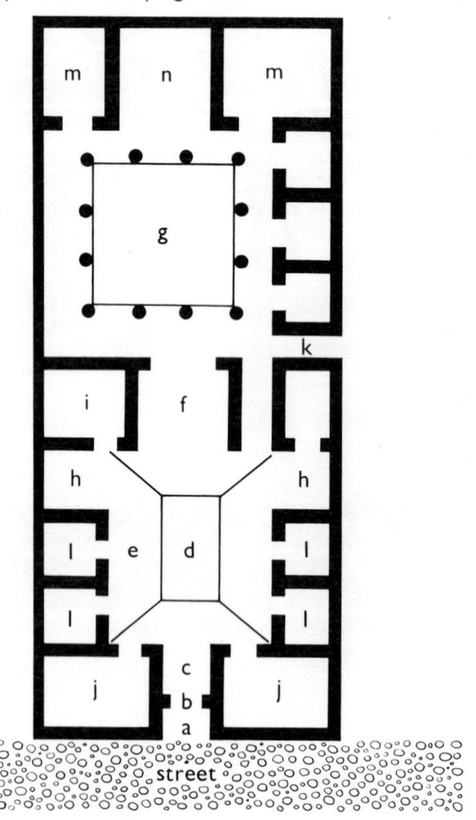

When you have finished, check your answers with the plan on page 46.

Now try the following questions

If you are not sure about the answer to the question, turn back to the page indicated.

	Question	page
1	Write down two ways in which the *domus* differed from the *cenaculum.*	17
2	What kind of person lived in a *domus?*	16
3	From whom did the Romans get the idea of the *domus?*	18
4	What did the Romans add to the early kind of house?	19
5	Why was the *domus* built in the way it was?	20
6	Why did the *atrium* have a hole in the roof?	23
7	How did the *atrium* get its name? What was it?	25
8	What was a *lararium?* Where would you expect to find one in a Roman house? What were the *lares* and *penates?*	26
9	What kind of furniture would you find in a Roman *domus?*	27
10	What could you look onto at the back of a Roman private house?	29
11	What kind of furniture would you find in a Roman dining-room?	32
12	How many people did the ordinary Roman dining-room seat?	33
13	What was the main meal in the day for a Roman? When did it start?	34
14	What would you find in a Roman *culina?*	35
15	Where would you find the bedrooms in a Roman house? Upstairs or downstairs?	37
16	What would you see in the *peristylium?*	39
17	Were bathrooms common in Roman houses?	41
18	Where did the ordinary Roman go if he wanted a bath?	41
19	What was the *posticum?*	41
20	Write down two kinds of decorations you might find in a *domus.*	42

Things to do

1 Make a wall poster comparing different types of Roman houses with houses today.

2 Look at the folder and find out more about Roman houses from the information sheets. F

3 Make a frieze showing the kinds of decorations to be found in a Roman house and a modern house. (You will find a model sheet on making a Roman mosaic in the folder.) F

4 Imagine you are a wealthy Roman citizen having a house built. Describe to the architect how you want the rooms and garden laid out and what kinds of decorations you would like. You could also draw a plan of your imaginary house.

Plan of a typical domus

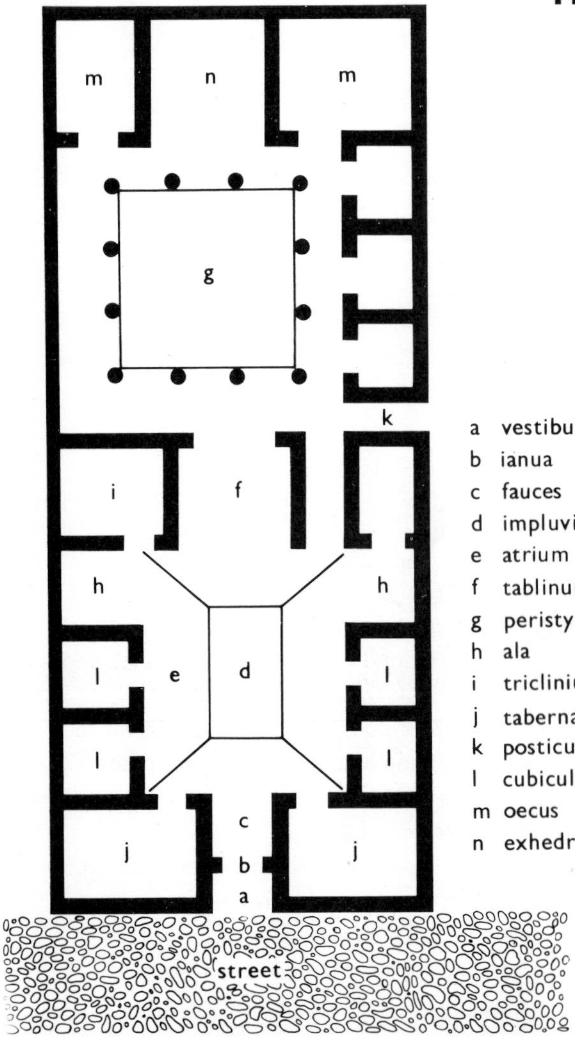

a	**vestibulum**	porch
b	**ianua**	front door
c	**fauces**	passage
d	**impluvium**	rain trough
e	**atrium**	room for entertaining guests
f	**tablinum**	living-room of the Roman family
g	**peristylium**	courtyard
h	**ala**	recess for the family busts
i	**triclinium**	dining-room
j	**taberna**	shop
k	**posticum**	side door
l	**cubicula**	bedrooms
m	**oecus**	guest room
n	**exhedra**	sun-lounge

4. VILLAS

The *domus*, as we have seen, was the private house which only the middle-class and rich Roman could afford to buy. The middle-class family might own a simple house of the kind shown in the plan of a typical *domus*. The rich merchant, banker, or government official, on the other hand, often owned a large, well equipped *domus* and might also be able to afford the luxury of two houses—one in the town and another in the country.
As the population in cities like Rome grew, and more and more houses and tenements were built, the rich felt the need to be able to escape from the noise and heat of the city and to enjoy the relaxation of life in the country and in the seaside resorts like that at Pompeii. It became popular and fashionable for the very rich to have a *domus* in the city, and a country house or **villa**.

Reconstruction of a villa at Lullingstone

Questions

1 What was a *villa*?
2 What type of person owned a *villa*?
3 Why did the *villa* become popular?

There were two kinds of *villa* or country house. At Boscoreale just outside Pompeii are the ruins of a fine **villa rustica** or farmhouse. It consisted of a dining-room, bedrooms, a kitchen and bathrooms, and a large number of rooms used for farm purposes—stables, a barn, threshing-floor for grinding corn, a wine-press for pressing the grapes, and a wine-cellar for storing the wine that they made.
Look at the plan below and find the rooms mentioned.

1 Triclinium
2 Bakery
3 Baths
4 Kitchen
5 Cow shed
6 Yard
7 Room for pressing grapes
8 Fermenting yard
9 Servants' rooms
10 Oil-pressing rooms
11 Barn
12 Threshing floor

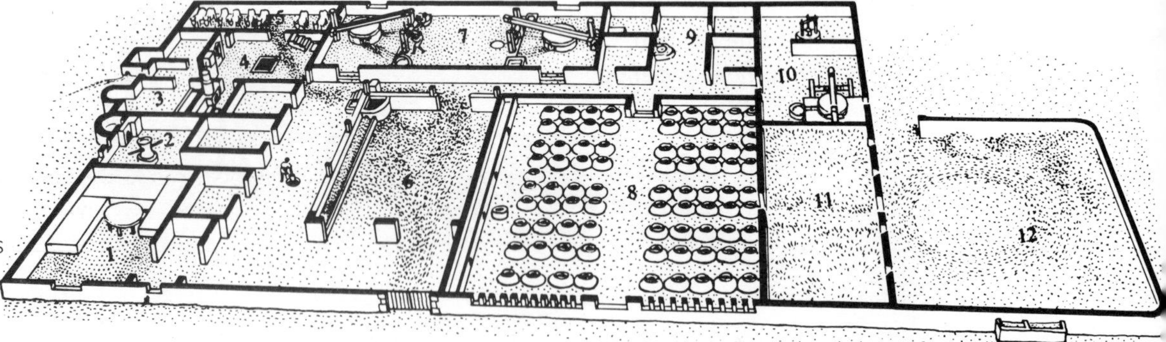

Questions

1 What was a *villa rustica*?

2 Write down the names of two kinds of crops you might find growing on a Roman farm.

The *villa rustica* was not a country mansion; it was just a farmhouse. In it lived the farm bailiff (*vilicus*) and the slaves who worked on the farm itself. When the owner wanted to stay at the farm, he would occupy a corner of the house.

The poet **Horace** owned a small farm at a place called Sabinum which is just outside Rome. Horace talks about his Sabine Farm in some of his poems. In the following passage, he is describing part of it to his friend Quintius:

'The hills are unbroken, except where they are divided by a shady valley . . . the generous bushes produce red wild cherries and sloes; the oak and ilex trees bring pleasure to my flock with large harvests of acorns and provide their master with plenty of shade. There is also a spring. . . .'

Later in the poem he describes a scene where he is talking to some of the farm hands:

'If a slave says to me, "I haven't stolen anything or run away," I tell him: "Well then, I won't have your hide flayed—there's your reward." If he says, "I haven't killed anyone," I say to him: "All right, you won't have to feed the crows on the gallows." If he says, "I'm a good and honest servant," my Sabine bailiff shakes his head and says he's lying!'

HORACE *Epistles* i. 16.

Questions

1 Where was Horace's farm? Did it produce much?
2 Who looked after the farm when Horace was in Rome?
3 Who did all the work on Roman farms?

A country house with colonnades, as shown in a wall painting

The other kind of villa was the **villa urbana**. It was a country mansion or stately home in the country.
Only the very wealthy could afford the luxuries of such a house, although there are several examples in Pompeii of the lavish splendour to which they went.
Look at the plan of Pompeii on page 4 and find the Via dei Sepolcri. (It runs out through the west gate of the city in the direction of Naples.)
On the left-hand side of the road there are the ruins of a large *villa urbana* which was discovered in the eighteenth century and is thought to have belonged to the great Roman orator **Cicero**.
We know that Cicero had a villa in Pompeii because in a letter to a friend called Atticus he says:

'I'm very pleased with my villas at Tusculum and Pompeii, except for the fact that they're ruining me, not with ornamental Corinthian bronzes but with the brass it takes to pay off the bankers—me the champion of creditors!'

CICERO *ad Att.* ii. I. II

Unfortunately, we cannot be sure whether this was Cicero's villa because Cicero does not give us a description of where it was.

Questions

1 What was a *villa urbana*?
2 What does Cicero mean when he says that he is being ruined 'with the brass it takes to pay off the bankers'?

Further on past Cicero's villa is another large villa called the Villa of Diomedes. In addition to the rooms to be found in the larger *domus*, it also had its own baths and a large *peristylium* and **hortus,** or garden, which you can see in the photograph below.
Notice the large pool in the middle and, at the back of it, the pillars of the summer *triclinium*.

Questions

1 What was a *hortus*?

2 Look at the map of Italy and the plan of Pompeii. What could the owner of this *villa* see from his house?

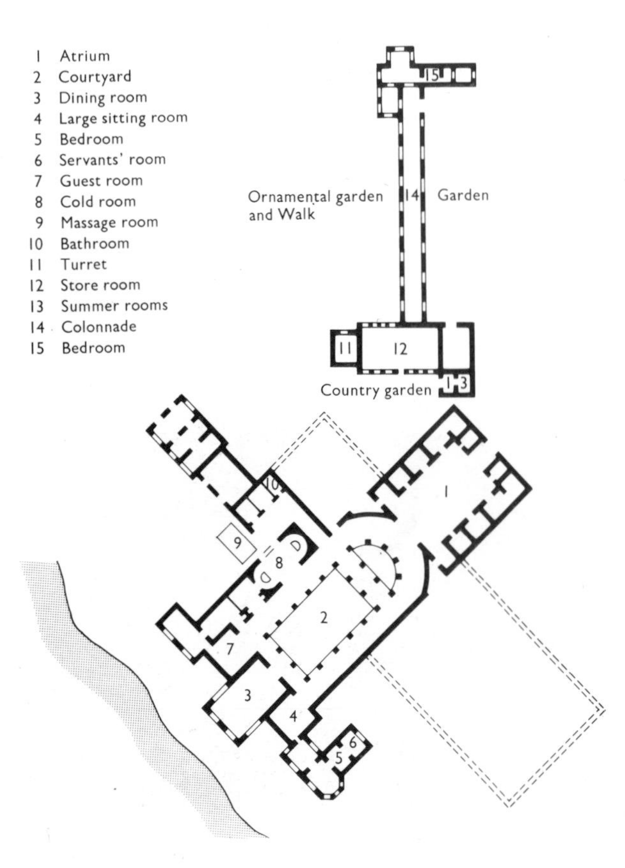

Plan of Pliny's villa at Laurentum

Pliny, whose description of the eruption of Vesuvius you have read in Chapter 1, owned two villas—one in Tuscany, and another at Laurentum which was on the coast just south of Ostia. Below is part of a letter he wrote to a friend describing his villa at Laurentum.

'It is seventeen miles from Rome so that you can stay there and still put in a full day's work in the city. The villa is large enough for comfort but not too expensive to maintain. In the front part of it there is a nice little *atrium*, which leads onto a *portico* in the form of the letter D and encloses an *open space* which is small but sunny. It makes a marvellous retreat in bad weather, because it is protected by windows and also by the overhanging roof. Opposite the middle of the portico is a pleasant *courtyard* and next to that quite a nice *dining-room* which runs out towards the sea, and when a south-westerly is blowing from the sea is lightly washed by the spray from the last breakers. All round the room are folding doors or windows the size of doors that give one a view from the front and sides of three seas as it were. Behind it one can look out onto the courtyard, open space, and portico again and through to the atrium, with the woods and mountains in the distance.'

PLINY *Epistles* ii. 17.

You will find the rest of Pliny's description of his Laurentine villa in the folder F, and a plan of it on the right.

Questions

1 Find the rooms mentioned by Pliny on the plan
2 What could Pliny see from his villa?

In the grounds of the *villa* there was usually a garden (*hortus*) and an ornamental hedge with a garden walk (**xystus**). Pliny's villa had both where he could stroll on a warm evening and enjoy the scenery. He also had a special dining-room for entertaining guests to dinner in the middle of the garden.

Below is a model (based on the plan on the opposite page) which shows what Pliny's villa at Laurentum may have looked like.

Pliny goes on to describe the rest of the *villa* at Laurentum in detail. One of the features he mentions is a heating system (**hypocausta**) underneath the floor; this was supported by pillars around which hot air from a furnace circulated, thus carrying the warmth into nearby rooms.

Below is a *hypocausta* in another villa which has been excavated.

A diagram of a *hypocausta*, showing how it worked.

Questions

1 What is the modern equivalent of the Roman *hypocausta*?

2 Do you think you would find this in a *cenaculum*?

Near the villa, Pliny says, were an ornamental pond (**piscina**) and a room where ball games could be played (called a **sphaeristerium**), rather like the modern private tennis-court.

Part of a mosaic showing a girl dressed for gymnastics (or possibly swimming)

Revision

1 What was a *villa*?
2 What kind of person owned a *villa*?
3 What was a *villa rustica*?
  a A country mansion?
  b A small farm?
4 What was a *villa urbana*?
  a A country mansion?
  b A small farm?
5 Which Roman poet owned a *villa rustica*?
6 Which Roman writer had a *villa urbana* just outside Pompeii?
  a Pliny?
  b Cicero?
7 What was a *hortus*?
  a A garden?
  b An ornamental hedge and garden walk?
8 What was a *hypocausta*?
9 Why did the *villa* become popular?

Things to do

1 Draw a plan of Pliny's villa at Laurentum from the plan on page 52
or
make a model based on the plan and the photograph on page 53.
2 Read the rest of Pliny's description of his villa which is in the folder. F Write a letter to a friend describing your 'ideal' house.

5. PALACES FOR EMPERORS

Although a few rich men like Pliny could afford luxury villas on the coast, not even they could rival the wealth of some of the Roman emperors who built magnificent palaces for themselves.
The Emperor Nero, for example, had a luxury palace built in Rome between 64–68 AD. It was vast and was surrounded by an estate with an artificial lake in the middle where the Colosseum now stands. Many of the rooms were studded with pearls and jewels and inlaid with gold—so much so that it was known as Nero's Golden House. Below is an artist's impression showing what it may have looked like. You will find a description of it in the folder.

Nero's Golden House, as shown in a reconstruction.

The Emperor Hadrian had a magnificent palace built at Tivoli about fifteen miles from Rome, the remains of which can still be seen today. It had long colonnades and courtyards with artificial canals, and was decorated with marble statues imported from Greece. It was probably built between 125 and 138 AD.
Here is a drawing showing what Hadrian's villa at Tivoli probably looked like.

Reconstruction of Hadrian's villa at Tivoli near Rome

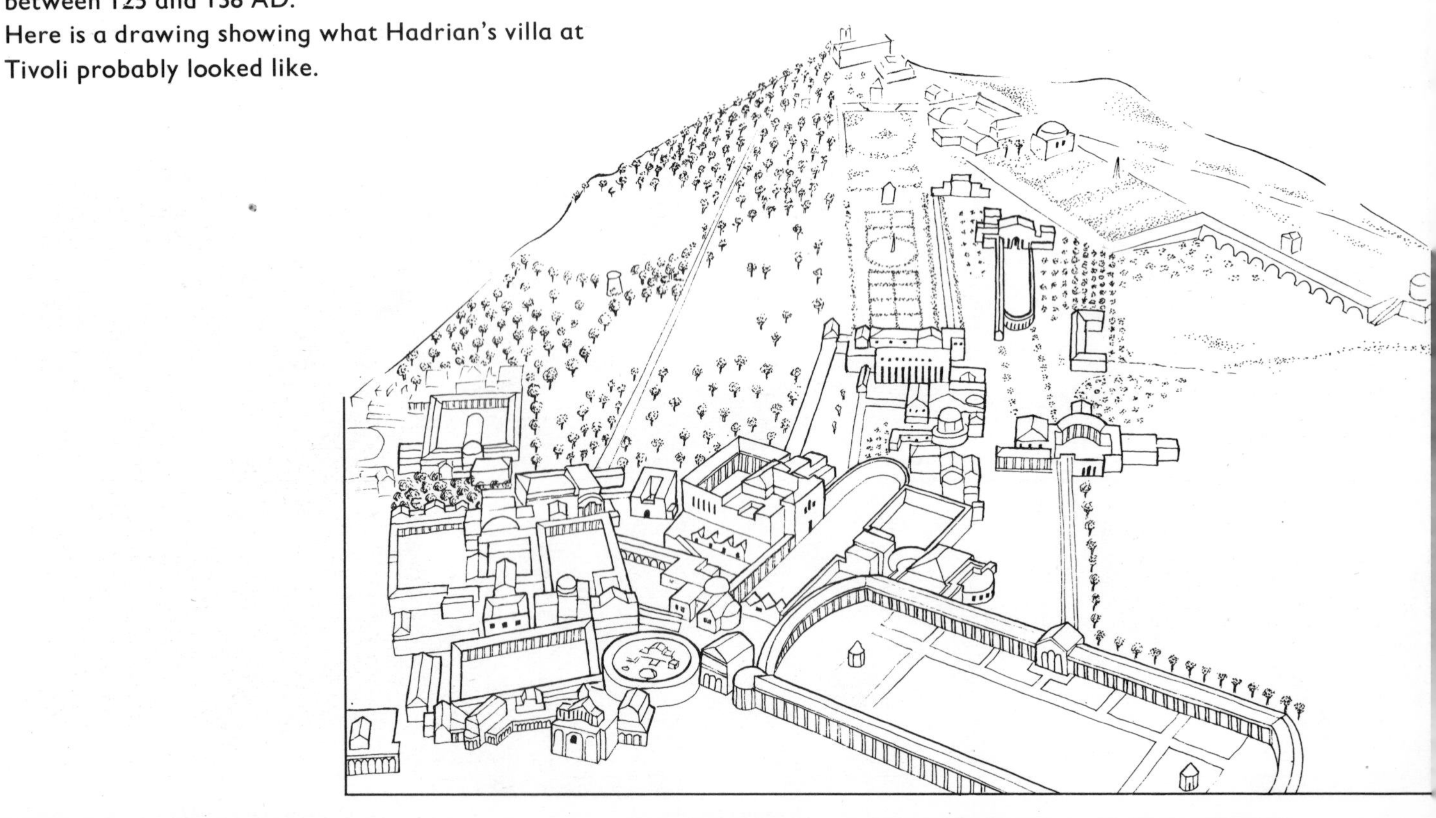

But of all the Roman imperial palaces, perhaps the best example to be seen today is the palace of the Emperor Diocletian which was built at Split in Jugoslavia about 300 AD. It was roughly 215 metres long and 180 metres wide, and covered an area of approximately 39,000 square metres. After the Roman empire collapsed a whole town grew up inside the walls of what used to be the palace.
The picture on the left below shows what the palace probably looked like in 300 AD. On the right is a photograph showing the town as it stands today. If you look carefully you can see the outline of the original Roman palace.

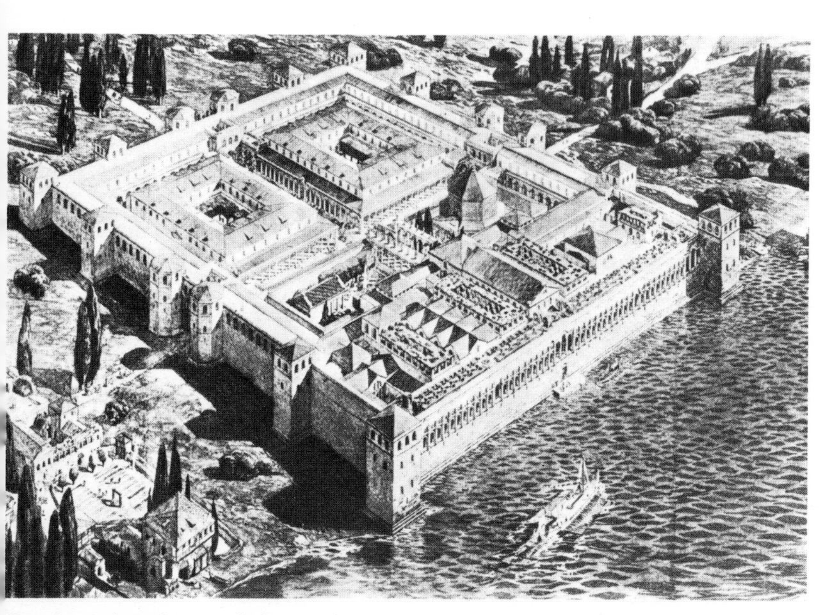

Diocletian's palace at Split, as shown in a reconstruction

The town of Split as it is now, showing the outline of the old palace

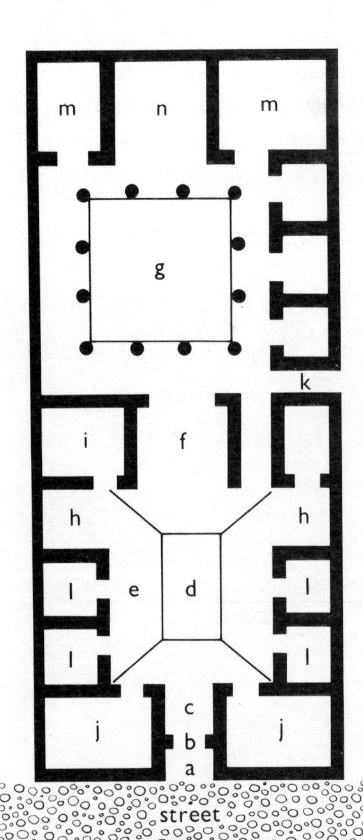

Revision Test

Do this test to check how much you have learned.

1 What was the disaster that befell Pompeii?
   a earthquake **b** flood **c** volcanic eruption **d** famine

2 In which year did the disaster occur?
   a 55BC **b** 79AD **c** 55AD **d** 79BC

3 What was an *insula?*
   a a house **b** a shop **c** a farm **d** a block of houses

4 What was a *cenaculum?*
   a a flat **b** a private house **c** a shop **d** a block of houses

5 Who lived in a *cenaculum?*
   a the poor **b** the rich

6 What was a *taberna?*
   a a flat **b** a shop **c** a private house **d** a farm

7 On the left is the plan of one kind of Roman house:
   (i) Write down the names of the parts marked on the plan.
   (ii) What was this kind of house called?
   (iii) Who lived in this type of house?

8 What was the commonest kind of house in Rome?
   a a flat **b** a private house **c** a mansion

9 What was a *villa rustica?*
   a a town house **b** a country mansion **c** a farm

10 What was a *villa urbana?*
   a a farm **b** a town house **c** a country mansion

11 What is the *cubiculum*?
 a living-room b guest room c dining-room d bedroom

12 What kind of house is being described in each of the following passages?

a 'We live in a city that is mostly supported on slender props. The house-agent patches the cracks in the walls and tells the tenants to sleep without worrying in spite of the fact that the roof is just about to fall on their heads.'

JUVENAL iii.

b 'It is seventeen miles from Rome so that when business matters are finished you can stay there after putting in a full working day. . . . Behind one can look out onto the courtyard, open space, and portico and through to the atrium with the woods and mountains in the distance.'

PLINY Letters ii.

c 'It turned a blind, unbroken wall to the street, and all its doors and windows opened on its interior courts.'

CARCOPINO p. 24.

13 Look at the photographs on the right:
 a Write down what each shows.
 b Write a short paragraph describing what you know about each.

14 Write a paragraph on each of the following:
 a the kinds of decoration found in private houses
 b the kind of lighting the Romans had

15 Where did most Romans have a bath if they wanted one?

16 a What kind of house is described in the following extract?

'It was so vast that it had triple colonnades a mile long. . . . Some parts were completely covered with gold and studded with jewels and mother-of-pearl.'

SUETONIUS *Life of Nero* §31.

b Who lived in it?

c What was it called?

17 Write a paragraph describing the kinds of evidence we have about Roman housing

Books to read

The following books contain useful additional information on Roman housing:

J. CARCOPINO *Daily Life in Ancient Rome* Penguin Books

F. R. COWELL *Everyday Life in Ancient Rome* Batsford

B. CUNLIFFE *Fishbourne* Thames & Hudson

H. & B. LEACROFT *The Buildings of Ancient Rome* Brockhampton Press

J. LIVERSIDGE *Roman Furniture* Routledge & Kegan Paul

U. E. PAOLI *Rome—Its People, Life and Customs* Longman

A. STENICO *Roman and Etruscan Painting* Weidenfeld & Nicolson

M. WHEELER *Roman Art and Architecture* Thames & Hudson